Quora

How to Generate Unlimited Traffic

DISCLAIMER

This eBook has been written for information purposes only. Every effort has been made to make this ebook as complete and accurate as possible.

However, there may be mistakes in typography or content. Also, this ebook provides information only up to the publishing date. Therefore, this ebook should be used as a guide - not as the ultimate source.

The purpose of this ebook is to educate. The author and the publisher does not warrant that the information contained in this ebook is fully complete and shall not be responsible for any errors or omissions.

The author and publisher shall have neither liability nor responsibility to any person or entity with respect to any loss or damage caused or alleged to be caused directly or indirectly by this ebook.

Table of contents

Introduction 1

Chapter 1: Set Your Profile 5

Chapter 2: It's Time To Answer 11

Chapter 3: How To Get Way More Traffic 21

Chapter 4: Curiosities About Quora 29

Chapter 5: Your Next Steps 33

Conclusion 37

INTRODUCTION

Hello and thanks a lot for your purchase, it means a lot to us. This guide was created to help you get thousands of leads in the next few months and get sales in the process.

We will use a special web 2.0 website, made to turn yourself into an influencer and leader and to exponentially grow your traffic over time.

Inside this website there are 200 million users, logging in every day to get answers to their questions and to help thousands of other people do the same. If you don't yet know the website we are talking about, well… it's Quora, at https://www.quora.com.

Now also available in Italian, Spanish and French to give more people the power to ask questions and share answers.

Quora is a second generation, powerful version of the good and old "Yahoo! Answer", that is now as great as it was a few years go. Quora is full of interesting contents for anyone, from marketing to offline marketing, from gardening to Star Wars and much, much more.

We're talking about 8.3 million questions and over 23 million answers in May 2017 alone, something humongous that will take an entire lifetime to be read.

Founded by two ex Facebook employees, Adam D'Angelo and Charlie Cheever, Quora has the mission to grow people's knowledge creating a never-ending quantity of questions and answers. Many famous people have left their comments on Quora, making it a valuable resource.

But we will watch it differently, as we will show you how to take advantage of it to grow your list exponentially, month by month. We are talking about tens of thousands of subscribers interested in your niche and ready to pay for your products at the same time.

But that's not all… Consider Quora best answers are visible on top of Google, ready to send you hundreds of visitors on a daily basis to your resources.

If you are ready to start, let's go!

Thanks a lot and see you,

Alessandro Zamboni

info@alessandrozamboni.com

CHAPTER 1

SET YOUR PROFILE

One of the best ways to start getting traffic to your URL's is to set up your profile with interesting information for whoever is checking it (and if your answers are good enough, you will have massive traffic checking it…)

So once you sign up to Quora, the first thing to do is to click your little icon on top, and select "Profile", or by using this link:

https://www.quora.com/profile/Alessandro-Zamboni

Where you will change Alessandro-Zamboni with your Quora username.

Credentials

Once there, there are a couple of things to do. First, select "Credentials" and enter your own credentials, or what you are good at doing. For myself, I have written:

"Author & Entrepreneur | Mentor | Influencer"

Depending on your niche, you have a few characters to describe what you do. Find a way to make it easy for people to understand what your job is.

Remember to add your actual and old work positions and the city where you lived and where you are currently living. These add more value to your profile.

Description

Then, in the second step, click "Write a Description About Yourself", and here you have to be really creative. What you can include is:

- Who you are.

- What are your best characteristics in life and work.

- Tell the best events in your life story.

- List your credentials, studies and victories.

- How you can help people.

- Offer something free in exchange for an email address (with a squeeze page.)

- Offer something paid with 20/30% discount (it works with anything that works with discounts.)

- Add blog, website, offers and video links, just to name a few.

- Add your social media links.

- Link your best Quora answers.

- Close with your greetings.

The text you enter in the description field supports bold, underlined and italic.

Remember that images can be added, so you can create something with Canva or Adobe Photoshop, just to name 2 of the countless software programs available to create graphics. It could be something promotional, like an offer, or a special discount, or a personal photo. Photos and images always add value to your profile, so add at least one.

Most of the users on Quora don't take the time to complete their profile, so by making sure you do it you stand a bigger chance of being more visible and getting more results when people go to look at your profile, and many are doing it. Me? I do it whenever I read a well-done answer and I generally add them to Twitter.

Remember that it is fundamental to add at least a freebie, and a paid offer to get a full advantage of this Quora method.

Here is my description, don't copy it but try to edit it to create something new and better:

I do internet marketing for a long of time, and have launched over 60 products on the market. 15 of these were chosen as "Deals Of The Day", with thousands of sales over the years.

<u>If you want to discover all my tricks, here are my best 3 webinar replays for you, showing everything you always wanted to know about product launching and selling. 100% FREE!</u>

If instead you want to have a look at my products, here are some of the best I ever launched:

- <u>Public Domain Empire</u>
- <u>Cookbooks Empire</u>
- <u>Cheatsheets Empire</u>
- <u>The Original Cheatsheet Generator</u>

- *[150 Ways to Earn Free Bitcoins](.)*

- *And much, much more!*

If you want to contact me, *you can reach me at my email address*. *I will be happy to hear from you.*

Last but not least, here are my links in case you want to follow me on social media, or just read the posts on my blogs.

- *[Follow me on Facebook](.)*

- *[Follow me on Twitter](.)*

- *[Follow me on Instagram](.)*

- *[Search for me on LinkedIN](.)*

- *[Alessandro Zamboni - Internet Marketing Blog](.)*

Thanks a lot and see you!
Alessandro Zamboni

Knows About

Always on your profile page, on the right column, there's a section called "Knows About", where you have to add your interests and especially things you know a lot about.

For example, I added these: Web Marketing, Affiliate Marketing, Marketing, Social Media, E-Commerce, Instagram Marketing, Instagram (product), Social Media Marketing, Internet Marketing Italy (my company), Blogging and Email Marketing. There's probably a lot more to my knowledge, but for me this is a great starting point.

When your profile is ready, complete and beautiful to read, we can continue to the second step.

CHAPTER 2

IT'S TIME TO ANSWER

Once your profile is ready, it's time to give our best answers to questions asked over Quora. This is a step where 90% of people go totally wrong, so pay attention to our process.

Now you have to find some best answers to see how to do the same on your own. To give you some help, here are the top topics on Quora for 2017:

1. **Technology** 31.7million followers

2. **Science** 28.3million followers

3. **Movies** 25.7million followers

4. **Music** 24.9million followers

5. **Health** 23.9million followers

6. **Books** 23.1 million followers

7. **Education** 22.6million followers

8. **Food** 22.1million followers

9. **Business** 20.2 million followers

10. **Visiting and Travel** 19.8 million followers

11. **Psychology** 17.2 million followers

12. **History** 15.6 million followers

13. **Cooking** 14.3 million followers

14. **Photography** 13.9 million followers

15. **Design** 13.3 million followers

16. **Sports** 13.1 million followers

17. **Economics** 11.6 million followers

18. **Writing** 11.4 million followers

19. **Fashion and Style** 10.6 million followers

20. **Philosophy** 9.4 million followers

21. **Mathematics** 9.4 million followers

22. Finance 8.9 million followers

23. Marketing 8.7 million followers

24. Politics 8.5 million followers

25. Television Series 7.6 million followers

26. Entertainment 7.1 million followers

27. Literature 6.8 million followers

28. Fine Art 6.5 million followers

29. Computer Science 6 million followers

30. The Internet 5.3 million followers

31. Mobile Phones 5.2 million followers

32. Current Events in Technology 5.1 million followers

33. Journalism 5.1 million followers

34. Physics 5 million followers

35. Healthy Eating 4.7 million followers

36. Science of Everyday Life 4.6 million followers

37. Entrepreneur advice 4.5 million followers

38. Nutrition 4.2 million followers

39. Medicine and Healthcare 4 million followers

40. Entrepreneurship 3.6 million followers

41. India 3.6 million followers

42. Startups 3.4 million followers

43. Money 3.4 million followers

44. Biology 3.4 million followers

45. Novels 3.3 million followers

46. Investing 3.2 million followers

47. Book Recommendations 3.2 million followers

48. Hollywood 3.1 million followers

49. Small Businesses 3 million followers

50. Writers and Authors 3 million followers

As you can see there are many spots that are bound to be of interest to you, with millions of people ready to read your answers.

Remember that your links can be placed not only in your description, but also on your answers. A good way to add them is by placing them towards the bottom 2/3 of your article, as many Quora users don't like personal or affiliate links at the top of text. Apart from affiliate links, an excellent idea is to add FB Pages or Groups links, your Slash group or your social media links.

Before choosing questions, surfing the web I found these to be the best qualities to ensure your answer is seen by thousands of Quora members:

1. A 7:1 ratio between followers and number of answers left by users. For example, a question who has 10 answers but 70+ followers, or 100 answers but 700+ followers.

2. A question with a lot of followers, as specified in point 1, but with many inaccurate or not valuable answers.

3. It must have an emotional pull, to tell your story. A question arousing emotions, starting a fire on conversations.

4. Questions with no images, or bad quality images, so that you can add a good answer with a few solid images able to stand-out, to be found easily between a lot of answers with no images at all.

Given these important factors, choose one category. In this example I will consider "Business", 9th for followers. In this topic there are, at the moment of writing, 162,200 questions. Pretty awesome! It is located here:

https://www.quora.com/topic/Business-49

Now have a look at the last questions, and see the answers with more upvotes. Check them to understand why they were upvoted so much. There's people getting 50 views per month to each answer, and others getting up to 5,000 and that's all free traffic for you if done right.

Check the angle of the authors who answered, how many words they used, if they used links and the language used.

Below each question in bold you will see three little dots. Click them and you will see a new menu. Select "Answer Later" to add all the questions you are interested in into a database, so you can write a specific answer when you have time, so you won't lose great opportunities. You will find them all by clicking "Answer" on top of your Quora profile.

Add them each and every day, and as many as you can, and you will start collecting many views of your answers, that will convert into clicks on your websites and consequently in to leads.

Focus on finding the best Quora users who answer the most questions and are always on top, and search on their profile for the topics they follow. If they are in your area of interest, add them. Check how they always answer right. Then search for questions which have a lot of traction, that have answers but are still not perfect, who have a lot of followers but still few answers.

But how do you write the perfect answer? Here we will try to analyze the characteristics of answers which became viral in no time.

1. **Personal Stories**

    Answers without personal experiences convert a lot less, so it's fundamental to add stories to each one of your posts on Quora. Readers want to imagine you in your story, so the more details you give, the more your readers will be able to imagine and feel a part of your story.

Remember also that if you can add stories talking about tragedy, bad life experiences, personal growth through struggle and more, you will capture the interest of people more than in any other case.

Add conflicts, inspire curiosity, share happiness and sadness, add benefits and let the readers feel a part of your moments. This is the key for becoming a top Quora member.

2. Don't Tell Too Much

Another important step you should take is to never tell too much, to avoid giving away all your best secrets in one post. Give away some hints or tips and tricks, and send the users to your other resources like free ebooks (with autoresponder form), blog posts, videos, podcasts and articles.

Let your visitors and followers reach your own places to know the rest of the conversation and don't serve them all on a single platter, because in this way they will be happy to click your links, and complete the steps you offer them.

3. **Use The Power of Photos and Images**

We love images and photos, it's not that big news. It's only the fact that sometimes we are lazy, and we don't add them to our texts or articles. Instead, especially on Quora, images give our readers the chance to read and upvote our answers instead of other people ones with just long and a never-ending text.

You can use your own photos, old or recent, or find images on the web on sites that allow you to use and share the images, like Pixabay, at https://pixabay.com, Pexels, at https://pexels.com, and Unsplash, available at https://unsplash.com, and so on. Add one every 200 words or so to let your post be visible, as others generally don't take the time to add photos.

But that's not all. Photos give a chance for your readers to imagine you in a specific situation, and to feel your same sensations. Let them be a part of a change you made in your life, or on something great you decided to achieve.

4. **Be Controversial**

   This is not to be done every time you write something on Quora. It is to use instead on a few topics where a personal opinion should be taken. Take a position, in that case, and defend it. Also if another 99 people say it's OK you can always be the 100th who says it's not. In this way people will look at who you are and start following you because you are not a sheep following everyone's point of view.

With these four things added into your answer, you will be seen much more better, and people will pay more attention to your replies than classic hit-and-run short replies that offer no value.

CHAPTER 3

HOW TO GET WAY MORE TRAFFIC

The first step to get more traffic is obviously by answering more questions, but never lose your focus, which is answering questions like no one else is doing, with much care and detail.

But there are also other ways we will analyze in this chapter.

1. Post Answers at The Right Time

To give you the best hour to post on Quora, you need to act in EST time zone, New York hour. The best two times to post taking advantage not only of US, but also of European countries and India, is to post at:

- 9:00 AM EST

- 9:00 PM EST

This way you can count on a lot more traffic than in other hours, because that is optimized to get your post seen by a lot more people.

2. Search Keywords

This second method should always be used if you want to rank on Google and get many more views to your questions, apart from being found on Quora and being found by Quora as an expert to answer more questions about the same topic.

You can use Google Adwords Keyword Planner, at https://adwords.google.com/home/tools/keyword-planner/ or MOZ Keyword Search, at https://moz.com/explorer. They are two good free tools, but in this example I will focus on the second.

I will try to enter "cryptocurrency", and we will see what comes out. Apart from an analysis of the keyword, below you will find "Keyword Suggestions" with a preview of 5 keywords. These will be enough to start with, but we recommend you to jot down a minimum of 10 keywords to target in your next answers.

So click on "See All Suggestions" to open a new page with all keywords available. Order them by clicking on "Monthly Volume" to know which ones are the hottest currently to target.

My 10 keywords will be:

- cryptocurrency / cryptocurrencies
- cryptocurrency exchange
- cryptocurrency mining
- cryptocurrency list
- cryptocurrency charts
- cryptocurrency trading
- cryptocurrency prices
- cryptocurrency news
- cryptocurrency market
- blockchain

In this way I also have ideas on what to search on Quora. Remember to avoid stuffing all these keywords into one answer, but use two or three per answer to give you the best advantage.

3. Trending Topics

Every day could be a good day for a new trend to come out. How will you know that? Easy, with Google Trends, at https://trends.google.com/trends/, Google Alerts, at https://www.google.com/alerts and Google News, at https://news.google.com/news/, you can stay informed about everything and join the conversation between the firsts.

First things first, don't forget to visit Google Trends on a daily basis, and go through the latest trends to see if there is something hot to talk about that could be interesting for your business. On Google Trends I get many news items I target in my cheatsheets, so you can be sure it's a very important website.

You can surf all the latest trends, or also enter your keyword to see how that trend is going, if upwards or downwards.

When you find a good and solid trend, add it to Google Alerts and Google News.

On Google News is pretty easy, you login and on the left column, at the end, you'll find "Manage Sections", and there you can add your keywords to target, like "new trend" and "new trends" just to give you two ideas.

Google Alerts is to be activated when you find a trend you want to take advantage from. You add it as a new alert, specifying if you want updates "as soon as it happens" or "once a day". Then you wait, and as soon as there is any news, you will get an email.

This way you have a 3-way system to find, check and manage all the new trends you can find. Consider I've been one of the first to catch the Pokemon Go trend and many others.

This way you can have fresh news when you need information to add on Quora, but you can also use them to support your writing and concepts.

4. [ATTENTION! THIS IS BLACK HAT!]
HOW TO GET THE TOP ANSWER

I've a new technique for you, but it is black hat. In short terms you risk your account getting shut down in a snap and there's nothing you can do to get it back.

You buy upvotes to get to the top of answers, so you can get a huge amount traffic if you choose a really good question.

With a lot of time spent searching I've found a good freelancer on SEOClerk, doing upvotes for you, this one:

https://www.seoclerk.com/Social-Bookmarks/528252/25-HQ-worldwide-quora-upvotes

It's the first with 120+ good feedbacks, and he's using all different accounts and various IPs to deliver upvotes, that are two of the best things. You can buy 25, 50, 100 or 200 upvotes for $2, $5, $10 and $20.

If you want to try this method, the risk is all yours. But in our opinion it is worth a try when your account has at least 5 to 10 answers given.

This way you will get on top and you will get a lot of visitors going to your URL's in the answer and on your profile.

5. Create an eBook With Q&A

As you are the producer of the contents you will add to Quora, at the end of each month or year you can copy all the questions within your answers and create a new ebook from scratch, or a Q&A membership.

This is easy, as you can access all your answers on Quora, or you can simply create them in a document and then copy and paste them on Quora.

You can add images to it or screenshots, and you can add all the affiliate links and personal products links you desire, as you are not on Quora, but you are giving away your contents.

The book could be sold on any marketplace, or given away on Quora for growing your list fast as a free opt-in.

6. Get Top Questions Research Made For You

This is a thing you can start doing when you get a good number of followers and when you have written at least 25/30 good answers on Quora.

Apart from looking at this Quora question that lists some of the top answers, finding a good freelancer is a priority.

https://www.quora.com/What-are-the-some-of-the-most-interesting-or-incredible-conversations-or-questions-on-Quora-that-youd-like-everyone-to-know

All you have to do is find a good freelancer to search good questions for you, with a lot of traffic and followers, or get the contents prepared by a freelancer.

In this last case, here you can get 50 high quality Quora answers on your account for $65. Remember to give your account details to get answers written via your account and not their ones.

https://www.seoclerk.com/Questions-Answers/563367/Guaranteed-Service-50-High-Quality-Quora-answer

Here instead is a link to get the best freelancers available on Freelancer.com that are able to do research for you:

https://www.freelancer.com/search/users/?q=research

Be clear with your request. You must ask them to pass you 50, 100 or 200 top questions with more than 500/1,000 followers in your favorite topics. The price should be less than $50 for the 100 links version.

And remember the 4 characteristics of golden questions that I gave earlier: a 7:1 ratio between followers and number of answers left by users, a lot of question followers, but with many inaccurate and not valuable answers, that it must have an emotional pull, to tell your story, and with no good images available on top answers.

CHAPTER 4

CURIOSITIES ABOUT QUORA

Quora has a huge community, and here are some of the best things you can do with Quora.

1. ANALYZING YOUR TRAFFIC

If you connect to this link:
https://www.quora.com/stats

Or you click "Stats" after clicking on your Quora profile pic, you can check statistics of traffic on your profile, to have a general view of the traffic your answers got.

You can see how many visits you have got in total, in the last 7 days, 30 days, 3 months or all-time. You also have the chance to analyze the results of each answer you left on Quora, to see the results you get and improve.

And apart from Answers, you can analyze Questions, Posts and All Content.

2. QUORA APPS

Apart from being available on the web, Quora is also available for Android and iOs platforms.

Here are the links:

Android

https://play.google.com/store/apps/details?id=com.quora.android&hl=en

iOs

https://itunes.apple.com/us/app/quora/id456034437?mt=8

This way you can also answer questions on mobility or just lurk around to get answers to your own questions.

3. GENERATING KEYWORDS WITH QUORA AND GOOGLE TRENDS

Apart from generating keywords for your Quora answer, you can also do the opposite thing, or generate your keywords for many purposes by crossing Quora and Google Trends.

Here is a step-by-step article by Neil Patel, one of my favorite bloggers:

https://neilpatel.com/blog/how-to-generate-long-tail-keywords-using-quora-and-google-trends/

It's very interesting and doable, and the results are really amazing. Give it a read and put this article in your favorites for future reference!

4 - QUORA RSS IMPORTER

At the following link you can find a Google Spreadsheet able to import the most recent and up-to-date Quora posts based on your favorite Quora category:

https://www.johnfdoherty.com/tool-quora-rss-importer/

On that page you can find step by step instructions, but it is very easy to use, and gives speed to your research jobs.

The advantage is that you can use latest answers for content curation, or as ideas to create more content for your blog, or for elaborating better answers to offer on Quora.

CHAPTER 5

YOUR NEXT STEPS

Now you have the keys to dominate Quora and start getting traffic, leads and sales through this awesome network. And in the process you will build a lot of content you can use for many other purposes, too.

Here are your next steps to follow to be sure to achieve big success on Quora.

STEP 1 - Complete Your Profile

82% of Quora users have a blank profile. This means losing all the traffic and interest you generate through your answers... So it's fundamental to complete your profile on your first day. Take your time, don't rush.

I needed a complete day to create my "Free Product Creation Webinars" squeeze page and email series, but I waited. When I finished it I added to my site.

Create your profile description on a blank text file, then copy it to the site when you are ready with all the steps.

STEP 2 - Start Lurking

When you go into a new place, the first thing you do is look around to understand how people act in that new place. Well, it's the same on a new web 2.0 network. It's a good idea to get to know the rules before jumping in.

Take your time and lurk around as a visitor. Add your favorite topics you are interested in, and start searching questions you have answers ready for. If you want click "Answer Later" and start collecting questions you have an answer for.

If you need help in finding solid questions, use the help of a freelancer that can collect them for you in an Excel spreadsheet, ready to be clicked and answered on your own terms.

STEP 3 - Answer Two Questions Per Day

Your minimum aim is to answer 2 questions per day in a good way. I generally do one in the morning and one in the evening as suggested on peak hours. This way in one year you can have more than 700 answers on the network, and this will turn into a huge and constant traffic flow to your squeeze pages, sites and social media accounts.

If you can do more, that's even better. If you can do less, it's good anyway to give a minimum of 1 answer per day.

STEP 4 - Final Golden Advice

Finally, always check your Quora account, and follow people who add you and add some on your own. Create a network of followers who are informed about your new answers.

Then, keep an eye on your profile, keeping your url updated and adding things to it like experiences, work updates, photos and so on.

Start sharing your answers on Facebook and Twitter as suggested by Quora right after you hit enter on your answer. Share your profile on other social media accounts and start generating curiosity.

These are the steps which will ensure your success on Quora. If you will follow them to the letter you can pile up to 300,000 visitors per month to your URLs.

CONCLUSION

Quora is a site that must stay in your favorites. It's one of the easiest traffic generation sources we have ever found online, and we didn't really expect so much traffic coming from it.

If you have any questions, or you want to send me your profile URL so I can request friendship on Quora, please send it to: info@alessandrozamboni.com

We want to see your growth on Quora!

Thanks a lot and have a great time,
Alessandro Zamboni
http://AlessandroZamboni.com

www.ingramcontent.com/pod-product-compliance
Lightning Source LLC
Chambersburg PA
CBHW030039230526
45472CB00002B/578